A GOVERNMENT "9-1-1"

"NEW BREATH OF FREEDOM"

William James McKee, Jr. 2016©

Food for thought

CONTENTS

ACKNOWLEDGEMENT

Over the years I have been most fortunate to have had many people who have given of their time and energy.

The foundations provided in The Virginia Plan, The writings of Thomas Paine, James Madison, Thomas Jefferson, and the work of many others are borrowed to be included herein; much of the work done in this document is of their ownership, not my own.

We are all indebted to our Founding "Fathers" for their valuable work, the federalist papers and the "anti" federalists as well. The framers of the Declaration of Independence and the Constitution were masterful.

We are all forever indebted and grateful to them. I therefore not only wish to acknowledge them but to dedicate this work to them as well.

Thank you

FORWARD

The author has brought together the recent difficulties and apparent misdeeds pervading our current government along with the historical work that is our present constitution.

In attempting to mold a system based upon the original constitution in intent and scope but extending it so as to attempt to forestall future misconduct and intentional flaunting of its effectiveness; new attention is paid to limiting discretionary actions and constraining authority.

While this work sets a high mark, it is difficult to envision it ever being accomplished given the present political climate in the United States and the reluctance of the body politic to embrace any change that would disturb their comfort and power base.

I fully expect that this is an exercise in futility but perhaps provides enough food for thought that it can, at the vey least, point our great nation back toward its original purpose.

INTRODUCTION

In beginning this treatise, borrowing the title from the words of Abraham Lincoln, seemed somewhat appropriate in the context of what he was trying to achieve at the time. President Lincoln served during a most trying time in our nations history and in moving to rebuild our country after such a devastating war, he sought to re-unite us, to rebuild us, to save us from the destruction that separation of the southern or any other states would surely cause.

We truly are a nation that while born out of conflict, has risen to the forefront of human achievement as to a citizenry governing themselves; not only successfully, but demonstrably better than those that have been attempting such feats for centuries past.

In studying the politics of the ancient civilizations, more contemporary ones, including those that exist today one sees progress being made for the benefit of the societies in general.

In the United States we have had the experience of having the founding of our present system of government prepare for the people to take part in the organization, the representatives they would choose to present and support their points of view; their wants, desires, and concerns.

It is most unfortunate that many of the people's representatives that attend the congress, in both houses, find it more desirous to attend to their "self" interests instead. Once a "politician" is installed; they are then engaged, not only in championing a cause, but also in constantly pursuing the means by which to stay in office.

They are certainly not the only self-serving people to consider in the making of a nation. The general populace unfortunately has grown to place their interest high above that of the nation. They urge their congressmen to bring home the government programs, contracts, and monies. Whether it is good for the country or not is not the question in their minds, nor is it in the minds of their representatives in congress.

How can we hope to succeed if we all want is for ourselves and to hell with anyone else? There are those in our society that are as coarse as rough-hewn oak. Few are the polished and benevolent in nature. Fewer yet are they that have the education, learning, clarity of thought and desire to work against all those odds to forge another Government and try again for a country that has a chance of success in the modern era.

History has reminded us that in the migration of people like the other animals and birds on the planet, adventurers seek new and richer surrounds. They set up communities and claim territories for their kind whether occupied by others or not; the idea of the stronger taking from the weaker.

Need we say that the politicians become the stronger and their constituents, the weaker? Without the use of physical violence and without the ability to enforce a time limit for

7

those who "serve" us in the Congress, what shall our course of action be?

Misdeeds abound in such a process and exacerbated by other misconduct and policies that, in retrospect, are harsh. We could spend years; in fact many folks have done so, in an effort to find past problems and grievances. Time to get over it; we can bask in victimhood or we can all understand that we can't change the past. It's time to move forward having learned a great many lessons about what to do, and not to do as we go. It's time to do this, together.

Migration is out of the question! Armed revolt is out of the question! If our only recourse is in the realm of the legal community and we are thus constrained, shall we not put forth another brave attempt at a re-writing of our Constitution with adequate safeguards built in and means to enforce it?

By a re-organization of our government to spread out the responsibility and dilute the "central" power cache along with well defined limited terms of service for our elected officials we have a chance to correct many past wrongs.

We can take a bold and decisive step towards a bright future for our posterity and ourselves.

We have nothing further to lose and a re-birth of a great nation to attend to; let's get on with it. Consider the work presented herein as a good starting point and we'll go from there. All of us, together, at last!

A NEW "NEW BREATH OF FREEDOM"
William James McKee, Jr. 2015©

If we look abroad we find oligarchs, dictators, kings, emperors, all-powerful clerics, military juntas and elected "Presidents-for-Life". There are tribal elders, warlords, generals with great dreams and armies to back their play for control.

Few are the countries with true freedom and liberties for their citizens. There are socialist, communist, fascist, republican, democratic, tribal, feudal, caliphates, and theocracies, to name a few. It boggles the mind to imagine the varieties.

So how do you take such a wide spectrum of citizens such as we have in the United States at the present time and successfully form a government that can provide for the security of the nation, offer the freedoms and liberties that we once knew upon the founding of the nation and keep internal peace amongst ourselves? The governmental system we have put in place has manifested within itself, a political disease that we must find a means of stopping and forestalling in future iterations.

As has been considered in the original founding of our nation, the persons placed in the highest offices of the land must be of an ethical, intelligent, and capable composition that is immutable. They must possess the desire and drive to press ahead and lead the government forward into a bright and secure future. There are those that must likewise be of intellect, ambition and inner strength in order to listen, consider, debate, and finally produce laws for the nation that preserve the rights of men, the freedoms and liberties of the people, and the sanctity of our security as a nation among nations.

Most unfortunately what has been recently seen is a president that wears the cloak of our President but acts more like a king or dictator. We find a congress that is hesitant, at best, to try and remove him from office or even formally challenge his actions. We find a Supreme Court that is substantially politically driven, thanks in part to the selection process itself. It even looks to the writings, decisions, and philosophies of other nations of the world when making their deliberations.

In sitting for a case brought by the Executive Branch or the Legislative Branch, we find that the court has actually worked to re-write the effect of, and intent of, the language of the legislation being challenged; Strictly a politically or ideologically driven re-writing of that legislation; itself an unconstitutional action.

Perhaps we must reorganize the fundamental governmental branches and make clearer the precepts, actions, legalities, and underlying body of documented struggles that hold our country together, or at least was originally intended to do. We have a constitution that has proven to the world that a people can indeed self-govern successfully although some flaws have been found over the many decades.

10

This country pulled itself up from the ashes of a brutal revolution and, most fortunately had amongst the populace, men that were educated, knowledgeable, and highly desirous to form a government to lead a new nation forward with the rights and liberties of its citizens as a paramount tenent. Perhaps a new approach is needed, strongly based on our past, and freshened with a new spirit of identity of the American People. We, as a single nation must live and work together if we are to succeed. The alternatives are terrible and reprehensible to consider.

Let's begin by trying to define the American citizens. We have the standard male and female of the species but we also have all the variations of individuals that one might imagine. It is not possible to cover all of the vignettes that are possible and it's not for a national government to try and manage such a task.

We have a society where many are not educated, many are highly educated, the vast majority are in between. There are many that, while without much formal education, are none-the-less very well situated in-and-of-themselves to succeed and help others as well. There are numerous examples of "highly educated"(?) fools and dunces; they can be found everywhere.

The national government has no voice, nor business, in trying to sort through such a variety. It has no business in attempting to educate the masses, nor to provide sustenance for them. It has no business trying to encroach into their lives and involve itself in local and specifically regional affairs (read: State's matters).

At best it might try to act as an arbiter with respect to conflict amongst the states and try to protect them from foreign incursions. It is possible for the national government to assist in opening up foreign markets for American products and investments. It is essential for the National Government to communicate with other countries, no matter the form of government they choose to adopt for their citizens.

The government must organize military and naval forces to protect its international interests and those of its citizens. It has the express responsibility unto the nation to secure its borders from invasion and uncontrolled access by foreign entities. Obviously we cannot be a nation if there are no defined borders, and for that matter, no definition of our citizens or their identifying attributes.

What exactly can the government do and for that matter, what should it do with respect to the citizenry and in developing a standard set of laws to try and organize the overall functioning of our nation? Can we possibly consider all the nuances that may manifest themselves on our young nation sufficient to then develop a set of laws that are meaningful and at the same time fair to all?

That is the task at hand and it will seem harsh to some, lenient to others, and untenable and immediately unenforceable, striking many with the desire to rebel and to essentially resign from such a society. We are such a diverse people that separation of one group from another would be foolish on the face of it. We must all find a way for it to work for all of us *together.*

A further study on the concept of "Separation of Powers", which has worked reasonably well to date, shows that it seems now to be wavering. In an attempt to further spread the separation and make the tasks much simpler for the Executive Branch, a fourth and fifth branch are proposed which will be responsible for the domestic functioning within the country. The Executive Branch can then concentrate on the international issues our country must contend with. All the branches will have an "Inter-branch activities committee" to work in close conjunction with and thereby promote greater harmony among them.

Since a great deal of the problems that have been found to exist seem to spring from the misdeeds of the elected officials; and much of that due to the idea of their continuance in office, a strict limitation on the various terms of service is presented wherein all "elected" federal officials shall be held to single terms of service. Such terms vary in time depending upon the specific position and function. This is generically known as "term limits".

For the sake of utility and consideration for the vast audience for which this work is intended, many details remain to be fulfilled by a companion treatise (appendix A), delineating the details with accompanying explanation and arguments considered in the final decisions presented herein.

It is with great reverence that the following text, verbiage, and approach, borrows extensively from its predecessors and the founders of our great nation.

Let's try and begin with the following:

THE NEW CONSTITUTION

PREAMBLE

WE, THE CITIZENS OF THE UNITED STATES, *in order to form a more perfect union, establish justice, ensure domestic tranquility, provide for the common defense and promote the general welfare do ordain and establish this constitution for the United States of America.*

WE *proclaim that we are a free and upstanding people in the International Community; that we will protect and defend our nation against all foreign aggression and threats from whatever source. That we extend the hand of friendship to all who would take it, but hold a "big stick" for those that raise up against us; and we further declare that the following constitution, herein illuminated, to be the voice of our nation, and of all of us together as one people, united.*

ARTICLE I: THE COUNTRY

The United States is a nation, indivisible, comprising the several states of our founding history along with the others, joined over our brief existence. It has territories across the globe in which it has interests and for which it is a protector. Other territories and lands may join from time to time.

14

The country and its possessions shall have well defined borders, inviolate, which the Federal Government shall enforce and defend from incursion, invasion, or endangerment of whatever sort from foreign adversaries and entities.

An attack or invasion on any of them shall be construed as such action upon the whole of the nation and shall be a cause for action.

It is essential that the states and territories work hand-in-hand to make smooth, the overall demeanor of the union. It is likewise essential that they all treat their citizens and visiting citizens alike with the respect and courtesy afforded to all citizens and families within the entire country.

The states and territories are to formulate their own sets of laws, rules, procedures, and statutes sufficient to ensure smooth and fair regulation of their region; but all-such shall be subordinate to, and not in contravention with, the laws passed by this constitution and the federal legislature, which laws they are required to enforce as the "laws of the land".

Any act construed to be of the "terrorist" kind, or giving aid, comfort, support, monetary assistance to, or is in communication with an enemy or subversive group or member of such a group by any person that is a citizen or who resides within the country, permanently or temporarily, if the charges are proven, shall be guilty of **TREASON** against the United States and the mandatory penalty is death or life imprisonment, in total isolation, without the possibility of parole; further, if such a person is working for the government in any capacity, they shall have a death sentence as a mandatory consequence for their action.

Any person that is seeking to obtain, is in the process of obtaining, or in possession of any documents, drawings, cyber information or any other kind or type of information or material that is classified at any level, from "confidential" to ultimate "top secret", or unclassified and pertaining to any work, research, or projects in support of government interests shall be guilty of ***ESPIONAGE/SPYING***; the punishment for such action is life in prison without the possibility of parole except in time of war, whether declared or not, when the punishment is a mandatory death penalty.

ARTICLE II: THE CITIZENS

The citizens of the United States are those that have been born to persons, whether residing within the country or travelling abroad, and who themselves are citizens of this nation; they shall have the status known as "Natural Born" citizens.

Other persons may become citizens of the country by application for citizenship, providing complete personal information, knowing or having learned the national language, that of American English, and having learned a prescribed amount about the country, its history, its governmental system, and its fundamental laws, rules, and specifics that may be of further interest. Having accomplished those tasks and upon examination by governmental officials, and having affirmed no allegiance to any other country, government, group, society, or entity, shall have the opportunity to take the oath of citizenship for acceptance as "Naturalized" citizens of our nation.

Further if any person adheres to a philosophy that includes rules or doctrines in conflict with the laws and principles laid out within this constitution, they shall not be welcomed or permitted to reside within this country.

While the citizens have rights and freedoms afforded to them by living in this country, they also have the responsibility to seek education and employment in order to contribute to the overall wellbeing of themselves, their families, relatives, friends, and society in general.

In a similar vein the citizens have the responsibility to ensure that the laws are enforced and that they themselves adhere to a lawful behavior for the purposes of the security and wellbeing of the community in general and for themselves specifically.

No special treatment in the courts or other law enforcement departments shall be given to a person or persons due to, or because of, "class", "religious beliefs", "gender", "sexual orientation", "race", "ethnicity", "country of origin", "personal philosophy", or membership in any organization or group; actions and behavior by such persons regardless of their personal eccentricities are required to follow the laws and rules of the country, state, and local governments as is the general populous.

The Citizens of the United States are imbued with the following "Rights" and Privileges that are hereby recognized and defended and held to be inviolate by the Government of The United States of America:

The right to life
The right to liberty; slavery in any form is
     prohibited
The right to pursue personal happiness
The right to be secure in their own residence
The right to freely speak their mind
The right to associate and assemble with
     friends and colleagues
The right and responsibility to defend
     themselves, their families, friends, and
     community from harm
The rights to hold, purchase, receive, inherit,
     own, and bear arms
The right to petition the government with
     grievances
The rights to earn, seek, gather, invest and
     hold treasure
The right to participate in personal behaviors of
     their own choosing
The privilege to be held safe from foreign
     enemies, foes, or invasion
The privilege to publish their ideas, thoughts,
     and information
The privilege to peaceful public demonstration
The privilege to move freely about the country
The right to resign their citizenship and leave
     the country
The privilege to seek medical aid
The privilege to seek education and training

The above enumerated rights and privileges are valid only if the citizen, in practicing them,

18

does not infringe upon the rights of others, cause civil unrest, speak treason or incite others to riot, break laws with intent, or cause others to suffer bodily harm through their words or actions.

ARTICLE III: THE GOVERNMENT

The government of the nation shall be one of a democratic republic in its form wherein the source of its power derives from the citizenry itself. The fundamental structure shall comprise five branches, those being the Executive, Legislative, Operations, Legal and Security, and Judicial.

The National government shall be known as a "Federal" government and shall have the responsibility to be the voice of the nation for matters, international; form, train, equip, and maintain military, naval, air-force, space-borne, a system of reserves, and national forces in order to ensure the security of the country, its lands, and its citizens.

It shall further have the responsibility to make laws consistent with the guidelines presented herein to provide a smoothly working infrastructure throughout the land, protect the rights of the citizens, and work with the several states and territories in order to maintain good relations between them all and help in forestalling as well as eliminating problems and disputes between them, and to promote their interests abroad.

It shall have the authority to enter into agreements and treaties with other countries, assume debt on the faith of the nation to repay and to extend credit on the faith of the borrower to repay the debt to us. For the purpose of providing these and other functions the government shall have the authority to lay taxes and levy fees and duties, as it may need to do from time-to-time.

The debts congress allows shall be repaid with a five (5) year period with whatever level of interest may be agreed upon. Alternatively a federal bond issue may be made extending to maximum of ten years; again at whatever interest rate as may be set at the time of issue thereof.

The states and territories, and each of them, shall be the source of the federal tax revenues. Various trade agreements, services rendered, or otherwise provided, and international dealings shall provide for various fees, duties, and payments to the national treasury.

The federal tax level shall remain at the level of the year preceding the ratification of this Constitution for a period of two years and apportioned as described in the appended description, while the more equitable apportionment is calculated and the rates set.

The Federal Government shall have the powers and controls granted to it by the States and contained herein. All powers and controls not specified shall be reserved to the citizens of the nation.

The states, while enjoying their own republican governmental system is responsible to the nation for its participation and adherence to the laws of the land and is therefore also responsible to enforce those laws as well as their own statewide and local laws that they may institute.

The states will assume the responsibility for the medical care, educational, retirement (Social Security or alternatives), and welfare programs previously carried out by the Federal Government. These programs may be continued, terminated, or changed as may be appropriate by the respective states.

All Federal Employees must be citizens of the United States with the exception of the uniformed armed forces. No federal employee union organizations shall be lawful or allowed. All federal employment is "at will" and as such may be subject to termination without cause or explanation.

All elected officials and principle employees, other persons appointed, including judges, justices, and those installed by the congress or heads of the other branches are subject to disciplinary or remedial action up to and including impeachment.

The Federal Government shall not provide health care, a retirement or pension plan, or bonus program to any employee as a part of their federal employment.

Federal salaries shall reflect the average wages of equivalent work done in the public sector. The heads of the several branches shall have their salaries set by law and may enjoy modest increases during their time in service if the national economy permits.

The line of accession within the Executive Branch in times of national emergencies and death or incapacity of the topmost leaders of the country is as follows: The President, The Vice President, The Secretary of State, The Secretary of Defense, followed by the remaining cabinet secretaries in their order of seniority.

The line of accession within the Operations Branch in times of national emergencies and death or incapacity of the topmost leaders of the country is as follows: The Chief of Operations, The Vice Chief of Operations, The Secretary for Interstate Operations, followed by the remaining principle Officers in their order of seniority.

The line of accession within the Legal and Security Branch in times of national emergencies is The Director of Justice, The chief of Homeland Security, and the remaining senior officers in their order of seniority.

The line of accession within the Judicial Branch is the Chief Justice followed by the remaining justices in their order of seniority.

The budget that the government works within shall not exceed the status of "balanced" wherein the annual expenditures shall be equal to, or less than, the incoming revenues for the coming twelve-month period. The budget may not exceed 12% of the annual Gross Domestic Product (GDP) of the nation; excepting times of declared national emergency or when war is declared and actions are being engaged.

Upon cessation of periods of distress, the budget shall return to its former modest levels of expenditure.

ARTICLE IV: THE EXECUTIVE BRANCH

The Executive Branch shall have the responsibility of being the voice for the nation in international matters. It shall form a group of "Offices" with which to undertake and control the various functions for which the branch is responsible.

The Offices of the President and Vice-President are elected offices. They are each installed for a single term of six years each; no exception is allowed.

The President and Vice President shall receive a compensation of $250,000 annually (2016 number) which amount shall be reviewed annually by the Congress ways and means committee to determine adjustments as may be necessary.

The candidates for these positions must be natural-born citizens of the country and must have reached the age of 35 years or more by the time of the election. All candidates seeking the offices must provide a dossier of disclosures and qualifications to the Chief Administrator of the Supreme Court at least 12 months prior to the elections for review and approval prior to being elected to office.

The "President" heads the branch and has a Vice President, Secretaries of State, Defense, International Commerce, Central Intelligence Agency, and The Executive Legal Affairs office.

In order to sufficiently organize such a number of offices the following is presented:

The Department of State;
The Department of Defense;
The Central Intelligence Agency
The Department for International Trade and Commerce;
The Department of Executive Legal Affairs;
The Committee for Inter-Branch Activities;

This branch is the international "face" of the United States and is responsible for all official international communications and negotiations.

All international treaties must be submitted and ratified by the congress prior to it becoming valid and enforceable. A 60% majority by both houses is required for approval of treaties. Agreements for international trade and other commerce must receive a 60% or more approval in the Senate.

This branch shall have a legal as well as an inter-branch committee to maintain close and productive relations with the other branches of government. One key area will be to ensure the legal standing of the various actions and activities of the branch with respect to our national laws and ratified and active international treaties.

The president is the Commander-in-Chief of the Defense Forces and, is responsible for the formation of the military, naval, air, space-borne, and system of reserves. It is responsible for all training, equipping, and deploying those forces internationally as may be necessary; in time of War or National Conflicts, and has the authority to require participation of "deep water" and patrol units of the Coast Guard to function under the auspices of the Navel Command.

The president shall not commit troops to naval or military actions without congressional declaration of war, except in cases of dire emergencies and when a delay is met due to congress not being in session, whereupon the congress shall be engaged in a solution within 30 days of the onset of any conflict so entered into. A vote of 60% or more of both houses of congress is necessary for a declaration of war.

This branch shall actively pursue commerce and trade with the international community of nations; seek to install and expand the trade opportunities for American products wherever possible; provide the means of locating and encouraging importing of products and services from our trading partners, and negotiating trade partnerships and agreements.

The President shall have the authority to issue Orders, regulations, and Procedural instructions specific to the Executive Branch but may not exceed to the level of legislating in lieu of congressional action.

Such orders, regulations, and procedural instructions are to be sent to the congress oversight committees for their perusal and legislative action if needed. If funding to support such actions is required the House of Representatives is responsible to put forth a bill for that purpose without undo delay.

The executive Branch has no voice with respect to pardons, commutations or other considerations in regard to criminal sentences.

ARTICLE V: THE LEGISLATIVE BRANCH

The legislative branch comprises **The Congress**, which shall be a bicameral organization with each house working in concert with the other to review current laws for efficacy and legislative action, if such might be required.

It is the responsibility of this branch to draft the laws of the nation, which shall be duly enforced by both the federal, as well as state and territorial law enforcement agencies.

The members of Congress shall receive financial compensation for their time in session, paid out of the Treasury of the state they represent. The amount of compensation shall be taken as the mean salary range of the citizens of the state they represent. This level of compensation shall be adjusted annually to reflect any changes in the amount to be tendered.

The House of Representatives is the enduring voice of the citizens in the government and is responsible for authoring all bills pertaining to governmental expenditures. It is also responsible for sitting on the impeachment of governmental officials.

The members are elected for a term of four (4) years and may not be re-elected for a second term. A person that has served in the House may not hold another seat in the Congress.

The members are elected by a popular vote of the people of the states in which they reside and for which they serve. The candidate's area of responsibility shall be distributed across their state within political boundaries established by the states as their "Congressional Districts" keeping in mind the population limits set forth therein.

The candidates must have reached their 25th birthday by the time of the election and have provided published their Curriculum Vitae for the public to peruse at least six months prior to the election.

No candidate may run that has been a member of a subversive organization, has been convicted of a felony, or any criminal conviction involving acts of armed violence, fraud, or having been diagnosed with a mental disorder. They must pass a security screening and exceed to a minimum level of "Secret Clearance" for governmental purposes.

Each state shall have a minimum or four (4) and a maximum of ten (10) representatives to serve their citizens and the population of the state shall determine the number of representatives. One representative per 150,000 adult residents will be the current ratio and shall be revised bi-annually to keep current.

The House of Representatives may also entertain a single representative from each of the various territories, and they may have the privilege of the floor but without voting rights.

The Senate shall be the voice of the several states. Two (2) Senators shall represent each state. The candidates for the Senate are elected for a single term of six (6) years. A person that has served in the Senate may not hold another seat in the Congress.

The members are elected by a popular vote of the legislators of the states in which they reside and for which they serve. The candidates must have reached their 30th year or more of age by the time of the election and have provided to the legislators, their Curriculum Vitae for them to peruse at least six months prior to the election.

No candidate may run that has been a member of a subversive organization, has been convicted of a felony, or any criminal conviction involving acts of armed violence, fraud, or shall have been diagnosed with a mental disorder. They must pass a security screening and exceed to the level of "Secret Clearance" for governmental purposes.

While the seat of the Congress is the Capitol Building, a separate office building shall be provided for the members of congress. The offices will be of a size sufficient for the members and four staff as well as appropriate furnishings and equipment needed to smoothly function.

Their staffs are employees of the states of which the member serves and whose compensation is paid by their states.

The senate may have a representative of the Executive, Operations, and Legal and Security Branches in attendance for their sessions. They shall have the privilege of the floor but without voting rights.

The **Congress** shall have the responsibility of forming the system of federal judiciary to serve the need of the nation in cases involving federal law. The congress will appoint the federal judges to serve in their appropriate districts and serve therein for single terms of eight years each. Such judges shall have monetary compensation equal to one and one-half time that of the annual average rate of congressional representatives and paid out of the Federal Treasury.

Congress shall select their respective leaders to preside over their day-to-day activities, select committee chairmen, bring bills and resolutions to the floor for consideration, debate, and the vote. These chairs are: a "Speaker" of the House of Representatives and a "President" of the Senate.

Congress shall convene for its business a minimum of twice a year and then for a minimum of two contiguous months. Absence from the sessions is permitted only due to medical emergencies and incapacitation or chronic illness.

All resolutions and bills proposed by the chairman of a standing committee, or by the other "house" of congress shall be brought to, and may not be withheld from, the floor for consideration and the vote without delay.

Bills drafted by any congressmen or senators outside of committee deliberation or requests for such legislation being received from the President, the Chief of Operations or the Chief of the Legal and Security pertaining to their particular branch's requirements must be submitted to an appropriate committee for consideration prior to being sent to the their respective house leaders for submission to the floor for debate and the vote.

The various committees shall hold such requests as high priority and shall address them for immediate consideration.

To ensure a smooth and orderly procedure, no hindrance or delay of presentation to the Senate or House of Representative floors is allowed other than by the author of the bill recalling it from consideration.

For bills to become law they must pass congress by a minimum of 66% of the membership of each house. Bills submitted to the floor of congress may not be amended or modified with content that is not of the same subject, substance, and intent of the original bill.

On occasion there may be a need to change a particular part of this constitution. This is possible using the amendment process set forth herein. The Congress, by a majority of

60% of its members of both houses may pass such an amendment which must be sent to the several states of record which must also pass it by a 60% majority in order for the amendment to thus be ratified.

An alternative approach is the calling of a Constitutional Convention by a state requesting, with 50% of the states of record concurring, whereupon a convention will be called; a notification of such a call is transmitted to the "Secretary of State" for each state of record stating the reason for the convention, the proposed solution by way of amendment and the date of convening which is to be two months hence from the date of the announcement. A majority of 66% of the states ratifying the language of the said amendment is then sufficient to have it thereby become ratified and the Constitution subsequently amended.

Yet another approach is for 10% of the voting population of at least five (5) states petition their states to request a convention, again stating the reason for the proposed amendment; again whereupon if 50% of the states of record concur, the convention is called as before.

The convention thus called by whatever method, should be held near the largest geographically located city having good transportation means and each attending state delegation and its expenses paid for by the states they represent. The convention is to be chaired by the second-most senior Justice of the Supreme Court.

Through appropriate legislation the Congress has the authority to:

- Review and remove outdated laws, rules, and regulations;
- Levy, collect, and adjust revenue rates on taxes, duties, and fees;
- Provide funding for the various authorized government programs;
- Borrow on the faith of the government to repay;
- Pay government debts;
- Review and modernize the national bankruptcy laws;
- Determine the methodology for immigration and naturalization procedures;
- Ratify or nullify treaties, which treaties must be in accord with This Constitution;
- Select, install, and have the power to recall any and **all** Federal Judges;
- Pass needed legislation covering federal issues for the country and territories;
- Select, install, and have the power to recall the Chief and Vice-Chief of Operations, Chief and Vice Chief of Legal and Security;
- Solicit the intervention of the Supreme Court as may be needed to compel action by the President, Chief of Operations or Chief of Legal and Security;
- Declare war, upon approval of 60% or more of both houses, or upon approval, by a similar margin, of a request by the President, Chief of Operations, or Chief of Legal and Security to do so;

- Pass legislation of conscription for government service during time of national crisis or war;
- Keep "Oversight" on the other branches of government;
- Work with the other branches to ensure the smooth running of the federal government and response to the needs of the states, territories, and citizens;
- Bar state and local governments, social, academic, professional, or religious organizations from passing any laws or rules to violate the rights and freedoms of citizens of the United States, and legal residents therein;
- Support requests by the President, Chief of Operations, or Chief of Legal and Security for legislation they deem essential for their branches to function in specific circumstances in lieu of regulations they themselves would promulgate;
- Invoke the power of impeachment against the President, Chief Justice, and other senior elected or appointed Government officials;
- Draft and pass any legislation necessary to improve and enforce the responsibilities listed above and those needed in the future;

Conversely, the congress does not have the authority to do the following actions with respect to legislation and amendments to this Constitution, Viz:

Congress shall not pass legislation:

- That extends to an "ex post facto" enforcement;
- Install a state religion;
- Allows treasury funds to be sent to foreign governments, businesses, organizations, or individuals except for legitimate purchases of goods, equipment, or services rendered;
- Levy's taxes on the income of individual resident citizens;
- Seek to negate the recognized "Rights" enumerated in Article II.

ARTICLE VI: THE OPERATIONS BRANCH

The Operations Branch comprises the various departments and agencies needed to maintain the business and order of the Internal "National" functioning of the Federal Government. It is headed up by the Chief of Operations and assisted by the Vice Chief of Operations.

This Branch comprises:
- The Government Accountability Office
- Human Resources
- The Government Records Agency
- Committee for Inter-branch Activity
- Department of Science and Engineering
- The Department for Interstate Cooperation
- The Department of Medicine
  - National Institutes of Health
  - Center for Disease Control
  - National Drug Center
- The Department of Transportation

- o Federal Aviation Administration
- o Federal Road and Highway Administration
- The Department of the Treasury
  - o The Security and Exchange Commission
  - o The Federal Reserve Banking System
  - o The Bureau of Engraving, Printing, and Coinage
  - o The Internal Revenue Service
- The Federal Communications Commission
- The General Services Administration
  - o Land, Building and Structures Division
  - o Mobile Assets Division
  - o Property Acquisition, Maintenance, and Disposition Group

This branch is responsible for the smooth internal functioning of: the country's interstate operations, nationwide infrastructure maintenance, the various properties and equipment of the government, the compilation and monitoring of all work related to the medical and drug communities, the setting up and maintenance of a full records department to include the archives of all documentation related to all government operations, all transactions of the federal government and comprising a triple redundancy system means to guard against any unauthorized access.

The Congress appoints the Chief of Operations and his Vice Chief. Their service is for a term of ten (10) years with the opportunity for a second term at the pleasure of the Congress.

The Chief of Operations and his Assistant must be Natural Born Citizens of the United States, eligible to hold top secret security clearance, and provide a dossier of their Resume' with disclosures of all memberships in organizations, and any criminal history.

The Chief and Vice Chief of Operations shall receive a compensation of $250,000 per annum (2016 number) which salary shall be reviewed by the House ways and means committee and adjusted annually as may be appropriate.

The Department of the Treasury is responsible for all financial transactions and dealings of the Government. The currency from the presses shall move into and through the "Assets Storage Group" facility on its way to the distribution centers located throughout the country.

The Assets storage facility works on a First-In-First-Out (FIFO) basis with the newest currency moving through the system as the need arises within the country.

The Federal Mint will have two active sites for the coinage of all current coin versions. The east Coast mint and the Gold Mint located on the grounds if the West Point Military Academy. All gold coin minting shall be done at the West Point location only.

All commerative and other short-run coinage shall be struck at the East Coast facilities.

The one and two-dollar bills will be replaced by coins of the same denomination and the penny shall be dropped from the minting process. All transactions in the commercial area are to be rounded off to the nearest $0.05. The present dollar and two dollar bills shall be legal tender for a period of two years after which they shall be dropped from their status as legal tender. Pennies shall remain legal for use but upon collection by any commercial or private companies, they shall be turned in to the Department of the Treasury for metal scrap.

ARTICLE VII: THE LEGAL AND SECURITY BRANCH

The Chief of Legal and Security with a Vice Chief as second in command head the Legal and Security Branch up. The Branch is responsible for all Internal Criminal Investigations, Security monitoring, issuing of Citizen Identification cards, Monitoring the status, location, and activities of foreign aliens, both resident and temporarily in the country.

It is also responsible for the arrest, arraignment, and prosecution of persons accused or suspected of breaking the law.

It is further responsible for monitoring all departments within the government via the Inspectors General Office, for all federal law enforcement departments and agencies, and finally the establishment of a "Cyber Security" Division, and comprises:

- The Department of Justice,
    - Office of the Attorney General,
    - The Office of the Federal Grand Juries

- o The Federal District Judicial Offices
- o The Federal District Courts, and Magistrates;
- o The Federal Circuit Courts on a District-by-District level;
- o The Federal Courts of Appeal on a District-by-District Level;
- The Federal Law Enforcement Administration
  - o The Border Patrol Service
  - o The Federal Bureau of Investigation
  - o The Federal Marshalls Office
- The Cyber Division
- The Office of the Inspectors General
- The National Security Agency
  - o This agency is responsible for Issuing Government Identification Cards and Passports to citizens and Issuing Government Identification Cards to resident aliens;
- The Secret Service
- Federal Port Authority

The Congress shall have the responsibility of forming a system of federal judiciary to serve the need of the nation in cases involving federal law. The congress will appoint the federal judges to serve in their appropriate districts and serve therein for terms of eight years. Such judges shall have monetary compensation equal to one and one-half time that of the annual average rate of congressional representatives and paid out of funds by the federal treasury. The system of the lower Federal Judiciary operates under the

Department of Justice within the Legal and Security Branch.

The Legal and Justice Branch has no voice with respect to pardons, commutations or other considerations in regard to criminal sentences.

All internal federal law enforcement and investigatory functions are to be absolutely devoid of political color or bias, pro or con, with respect to a persons ethnicity, religion, race, level of education, status or prominence or position in the community or membership in any particular group or organization.

ARTICLE VIII: THE JUDICIAL BRANCH

The Judicial Branch comprises the Supreme Court of the United States, which shall be the highest judicial authority of the nation. The Chief Justice and the Chief Administrator of the Court head it.

There shall be nine justices; the most senior shall be the Chief Justice responsible for the coordination and assignments of the various judicial tasks involved in the judicial processes.

Each justice is chosen by a minimum two-thirds vote of the senate judicial committee and serves for nine (9) years. Each year another justice is selected and the chief justice's term of service ends. The terms shall run from February 1st to the following February 1st of each year.

The Chief Administrator of the court is likewise appointed by the congress and serves for a term of eight years. He is responsible for the overall administrative functioning of the court in support of the justices and their judicial responsibilities.

The court comprises:

- The justices and their personal staff
- The office of the Chief Administrator and personal staff
- The office of Inter-branch Activity
- The clerical department
- The library and research department
- The court security Department

The Supreme Court has the responsibility for hearing cases brought to it concerning the application of the federal laws upon which the plaintiff's argument is based.

The justices are reminded that they are arbiters and not legislators. For all purposes of their deliberations, the justices shall use the Constitution and all ratified current treaties as the "law of the land" and no other source shall be held as valid. All decisions shall be without political color or the personal passion, likes, or dislikes of the justices.

For cases between the several states or territories, the court has primary responsibility. For cases between the several branches that are of a constitutional nature, the court also has primary responsibility. For cases between citizens and other citizens or the several states or territories it has secondary responsibility subsequent to being referred by the lower federal court system.

In any case between the branches, states, or territories, when settled by a simple majority of the court, the congress, in the person of the leader of either house, may request a stay of the decision pending review of the laws subtending the decision and the possibility of remedial legislation to be considered to address the original complaint. Such a stay may be in effect for up to a six (6) month period while congress deliberates and prepares remedial legislation.

Another responsibility is for their "inter-branch activity" department to work closely with the other branches in an advisory capacity, as well as having the responsibility of vetting of the various candidates for federal office prior to elections and addressing any formal challenges to the accreditation subsequent to the elections if new information has been discovered that warrants a new evaluation.

During the inauguration of the newly elected President, the Chief Justice shall administer the oath of Office. The second-most senior justice shall preside over any constitutional convention that may be convened by The Congress or upon being called by the several States.

During the trial phase of an impeachment process within the congress the Chief Justice, if not the person subject of the impeachment proceedings, shall preside over the senate when it is sitting in judgment of the impeachment.

APPENDIX:

A. ARGUMENTS AND EXPLANATIONS FOR THE NEW CONSTITUTION AND GOVERNMENTAL APPROACH

In view of the details presented herein and with respect to those persons that may go so far as to read the initial piece presenting a "NEW" government concept and accompanying constitution but would be overwhelmed by a further explicatory exercise. I intend to present arguments and rationale in support of the approach previously presented.

In the preamble the reference is specifically to the "Citizens", not the "People" since the fundamental issues are intended for citizens alone. If others reside within the Country, either on a permanent or temporary basis, they are subject to very much the same laws, rules, and regulations, but are under a slight difference as to their rights, obligations, and privileges while residing within our country.

The intention of this document and its ratification is for the people as a whole, not separate factions, not different groups, religions, colors, ethnicity, sexual persuasion, gender, or the like, but ONE PEOPLE, together, as citizens together, living in one nation, together.

Obviously we are all in need of finding a way wherein we can all contribute to our society, be recognized by our fellow citizens, and be respected as the individuals we are.

I realize that the work I have done here is sophomoric and in large part the attempt by a person not broadly educated in the ways of legal documents or political intrigues. Some of that is intentional in the hopes that many of our everyday citizens would have a look and understand this new approach and the benefits that might be derived from it.

Hopefully some intelligently educated people that may happen by, will peruse it and take an interest in trying to help reshape our country in a manner more like that young nation from over two hundred years ago that fought, struggled, and started a government experiment that surpassed all others on the earth.

I don't have the influence, the education, or the experience to do any sort of final attempt at this work. I need help with it, perhaps more ideas, perhaps simply to begin the process and watch where it leads.

In that sense I therefore submit the following as a first attempt at a new constitutional approach strongly borrowing from our founders. With incorporation of many modifications and amendments installed over time, and adding still further changes in order to bring a clearer idea of the intricate relationships between the people, the federal government, the state governments and the interworking between them.

It must be understood that when changes are made and we begin to rebuild our country anew, enforcement of the new constitution must be instilled in the leadership from the beginning. It almost goes without saying, or at least it should, that our present Constitution would still be a functional instrument if its provision were enforced, as they should have been.

IT IS IMPERITIVE TO NOTE THAT THIS PLAN DOES NOT SUGGEST VIOLENCE, ANARCHY, CIVIL UNREST, OR MILITARY COUP, BUT CONSIDERED, CONCERTED, AND ORDERLY ACTION BY THE CITIZENRY IN ORDER TO SAVE WHAT WE HAVE; NOT DESTROY IT.

IT IS IMPORTANT THAT ALL POTENTIAL AGGRESSORS AND USURPERS BE STRONGLY ADVISED TO WITHHOLD ANY ACTIONS AGAINST THIS NATION DURING THIS FORMATIVE PERIOD. ANY SUCH ACTION SHALL BY MET WITH AN IMMEDIATE AND DEVASTATING RESPONSE BY OUR MILITARY AND LAW ENFORCEMENT FORCES WITH PREJUDICE.

Without question the proposed approach will cause great consternation within the ranks of Congress, Political Parties, and the vast multitude of government employees but a peaceful "purge" and a full "do over" is needed in order for this work to succeed. I beseech all people involved to work for the common good here. We will end up with a new, stronger, and better nation.

I RECOMMEND A TERMINATION of the present congress, supreme court and presidency; And that the functions of those governmental bodies be led by a council comprising two (2) select, well-educated, non-politically aligned, representatives from each state. Let's call it

the "Interim Governance Council" that will have
a brief and finite existence while awaiting the
formation of the newly formed and refreshed
Democratic Republic government such as the
one that had served us so well over the past
250 years. This "Governance Council" may use
the present United States Senate Chamber,
presently arranged to support seating and
secure work environment for their purposes.

This action is to be concurrently accomplished
with the formation of a constitutional
convention comprising a similar Council of
three (3) similarly qualified representatives
from each state, to review the proposed
document, modify it as they may find desirable,
and then upon passage by a majority of 66% or
more of the membership thereof, ratify and
install the new constitution as the law of the
land.

While it would be desirable to have
representatives from all ethnic, racial, and
gender groups involved, that may not be
probable and it will fall to all those actually
selected to include ALL citizens in their
thoughts and actions as they go through the
process. You will represent the country as a
whole for the good and benefit of all of its
citizens.

It is not the time to consider the aberrations
and ner-do-wells of society; that bridge will be
crossed upon completion of the present task at
hand.

The above action is not intended to remove the
constitutional form of government we have
embraced for these past centuries but instead

to remove the fundamental corruption that has found its way into the system and to circumvent future similar incursions.

In order for anarchy to be stayed from this proposed work and in order to continue the fundamental business of government, the current departmental cabinet secretaries shall remain in place and work "hand-in-glove" with the newly formed "Interim Governance Council" to continue the basic and essential operations of their respective departments.

The Joint Chiefs of Staff of our armed forces and the Commandant of the Coast Guard will remain in place, the secretary of defense shall work with them, and the joint chiefs and the Commandant of the Coast Guard shall continue top-level command of their respective forces during this transitional period.

No state or local governments will have changes impressed upon them pending the issuance of a new constitution when put in place; nor shall their status as states of this union change. The union shall be preserved, as it exists at present. An evaluation of our present system and movement towards increased "States Rights" and a significantly lesser role for the "Federal Government" is the direction of intent.

The idea or a central (Federal) government that was to work with the states instead of "dictating" to them must be renewed and modified to bring us back together as willing and accepting partners in our quest for a coalesced and stronger nation.

It is essential that all standing Executive/Presidential orders be suspended and their contents evaluated so as to be included within or excluded from the text of The New Constitution.

The time period for review, submission of proposed changes, arguments for and against, and the final drafting of this constitution should be in no more than six months and must be completed, prepared and promulgated within twelve months of the onset of this effort. Any delays beyond this time limit would most likely morph into a permanent stage for continuous argument and disharmony; eventually a destructive force and invitation to anarchy and disaster.

For the purpose of convening a Constitutional Convention in the modern sense, permit the following to be considered as guidelines for the task.

This convention shall comprise delegates from each state, which delegates are to be chosen from the ranks of citizens that have participated in the federal elective process (cast votes) for at least the past five years, are not, and have not been aligned with a political party and that have reached the age of at least 50 years.

The proposed term for the convention to accomplish its work is up to six (6) months. The delegates shall be compensated for their work subsequent to the ratification of the new Constitution, and that compensation paid out of the Treasury of the United States. The compensation should be set at $200,000 for the term in appreciation of their sincere and diligent efforts.

The venue for the Convention might be a place like the Greenbrier in West Virginia due to its facilities, location, history, and accommodations. The Delegates should be reasonably sequestered. The site shall be made secure and a full medical team with facilities shall be "on-call" during the full length of the convention's deliberations. A supporting secretarial and administrative staff shall be available for the entire duration as well as a cafeteria.

The full proceedings shall be recorded on video for the archives and general distribution subsequent to the close of the convention.

Any interested "media" and other curious persons should be kept apart from them, with a "stream" of information and weekly reports being provided to them by the office of the Convention Secretary. A monthly "Press Conference" may be desirable in order to suggest the progress being made and to have them become a supportive part of the process in general.

It is suggested that the delegates only have contact with their families outside of the complex and that they themselves refrain from allowing their attentions and concentration to be diverted by the use of electronic devices such as radio or television; the playing of music excepted.

Each delegate will have clerical assistance provided to each of them to aid them in compiling notes, suggestions, questions, and maintaining a general ledger chronicling their activities for posterity.

It is proposed that a President and a Secretary for the Convention be chosen and that they have a clerical team to assist them in the operations of the convention. It is also recommended that the following approach be considered for organizing the initial meeting. The delegates shall all be given a portfolio containing the original "Declaration of Independence", the original "Constitution of the United States" and the new version of the "Constitution of the United States", with attached "Appendix".

Upon bringing the convention to order one week later, having given the delegates that brief time period in which to peruse the contents of the portfolio, the delegates will review the "new" constitution in a familiarization session; not to agree, approve, disapprove, or recommend changes but instead to simply affirm their understanding of the document and the approach for the new government structure.

This review and discussion will be given a full week of one-half day morning sessions with the remainder of the time given the delegates to consider to sessions proceedings and formulate any questions meant to clarify any confusion that may have arisen.

After this first two-week period is up, the convention needs to begin its intensive study and deliberations as to the articles; specifically those attempting to define the country, the citizens, the government in general and miscellaneous items of interest apart from specifics concerning any of the articles concerning the "branches" in particular. This portion of the effort should take no more than two calendar weeks to accomplish.

Upon completion of that "general" structure session, the delegates will be asked to fill out a short form with the following information:

- o   Their name and;

- o   The order of their interests in the several branches and;

- o   Indicating thereby, in which particular branch of the proposed government they would prefer to participate during the intensive sessions yet to follow.

It is recommended that the delegates then be assigned to their "Branch Committees" with their preferences being considered in the selection process. Each committee shall have 29 delegates assigned to it. The remaining five shall be the Convention President, Secretary and three Alternates to replace any committee members that are unable to continue, either briefly or as a permanent member of the committee.

Each "committee" shall choose a chairman and a secretary and then organize among themselves as may be conducive to proper attention being given to various areas of work within their particular branch's structure and responsibilities. It is suggested that a full and informal committee "gathering" take place for a brief period at the end of each calendar week to socialize, chat, and relax from the week's intense efforts.

It is further suggested that an "Executive" committee comprising the President, convention secretary and the several committee chairmen be formed with the intent of providing brief weekly progress reports and addressing any pressing general convention issues.

If one branch completes its work before the others, its members may then retire from the intense efforts and assist in whatever tasks they themselves may find available to participate in if they so wish; remaining on-site and still obliged that they are an active delegate to the convention in-progress.

The maximum length of time for the convention to accomplish it's task is proposed to be six (6) months; If the task is completed before that term, so much the better.

The final task for the delegates shall be the bringing together of the completed articles for which the convention has labored and compile them into a "completed" constitution whereupon they shall again review it to appreciate the extent of results of the labors their fellow delegates have endured in order to accomplish their tasks.

The final task of the convention delegates shall be that of "Ratifying" the New Constitution and Governmental Organization by a vote. For the purpose of ratifying, the vote "For" must reach a minimum level of 66 percent of the delegates. Several iterations may be done to achieve this goal if necessary.

Upon ratification, the Convention President shall have the clerical staff provide 500 serial numbered official copies, with appropriate seals, and signatures affixed thereto.

The delegates shall be dismissed with gratitude for their good work and the copies of the ratified constitution sent with appropriate cover letters to the several states and the national archives.

A further dissemination of some of these copies is for a personal copy for each delegate, one for each territory, and for those most senior federal officials that have remained at their posts during the transition.

The process of the formal transition of the government organization shall begin within a month's time and move with intent and deliberation to be accomplished within a period of eighteen (18) months. Some of the various portions of the governmental responsibilities such as legal, financial and Federal-State re-organization may extend outward for an additional year if need be.

For purposes of background and explanation, please permit the following rationale and arguments to be considered.

In *Article I* (*THE COUNTRY*) we find an attempt to define the country as the contiguous states of our heritage along with the other states, as well as the various territories, possessions, and protectorates.

The territories, possessions and protectorates are recognized as being in a temporary situation and subject to evolving or being changed by outside influences into another identity. Some may apply for statehood, some for complete dissolution of political and governmental attachments, and the like.

It is important to pronounce that the borders of the nation, by which we are physically defined, are laid out for identification. It is equally necessary that we declare that we will defend ourselves and the borders involved using whatever force and intensity as may prove to be necessary.

For all purposes the borders shall be thought of as a solid barrier of infinite height and held impervious from incursions by use of force. This includes any person, group, craft, or mechanism that may cross a border without permission or invitation by a governmental official.

We move to the idea that it is necessary for each of the states of the union, the various territories, possessions, and protectorates work in conjunction with one another in an effort to ensure that we all subsist well within our country and for the good and wellbeing of each other. While we embrace all the citizens who abide with us, the borders and gates are open for them to depart and resign their status as citizens.

Understand that we are not a "white" nation, nor "black" nor "Asian" nor "Hispanic"; we are not Christian, Buddhist, Jewish, Hindu, Shinto, Baha'i, Muslim, or other specific religion, but recognize that all exist within our borders. Our laws must belong to all of us together. While we have extracted much of our legal system from the English System historically and have taken much of our moral and behavioral doctrine from the Judeo-Christian values of the past, we have no "State" religion nor ascribe ourselves to any.

Our laws and rules of conduct must embrace all of us and none shall be put aside other then those that do not join in abiding by those laws. If one's personal philosophy is in opposition to our laws and rules, they must put their philosophical system as submissive to ours or remove themselves from our country. No acts disrespecting our laws in favor of another legal or philosophical system can be tolerated; the perpetrator must be removed from within our society permanently.

In Article II (THE CITIZENS) the idea of "Citizens" is addressed with a differentiation being made between the "natural-Born" and "naturalized" citizen. The distinction is made for the purpose of dealing with the qualifications obligatory for the highest governmental positions and for no other purpose. No distinction as to general government-citizen relationship, benefits, treatment, discrimination, or penalties, ascribe to the "naturalized" status of an individual.

One is reminded that while enjoying the benefits of residing in this great nation, one is expected to behave within the bounds of civility and in accordance with the laws, rules, and statutes of the country and region in which they reside. Not only is one supposed to be thus observant but to instill in their family, friends, and acquaintances, to comport themselves likewise.

There are always going to be those people that are mal-contents, troublemakers, or less than enthusiastic about taking care of themselves and push upon others to be stewards for them. If such people can't or wont leave of their own accord and still want to remain citizens but wish such caretaker treatment, they will have to accept private charities that our very compassionate citizens so often demonstrate. The state, or region in which they are residents may provide some level of assistance, training, consultation, or other services but no federal monies will be made available for welfare programs.

It is, of course, necessary for the states, territories, and possession to draft sets of laws by which they can govern their regions effectively. While they are subject to the fundamental laws covered by our constitution the states, etc. they will need laws, rules, statutes, and procedures that are specifically designed for their particular needs.

In our past experiences with governing we found occasions wherein some state would tend toward extremes and indeed treat citizens as if they were aliens; they are all citizens of the United States and shall be treated as respectfully as conditions and their behavior allow. The states are reminded that we must

all work together for a stronger sense of unity
and preservation of human dignity.
Oppression has no place in our society;
persons that believe they have been subjected
to it by their state should pursue the matter in
the courts.

Perhaps a harsh and "to-the-point" statement
would be appropriate here; the border is not
closed for those that do not want to be a
productive, supportive, and hard working
member of this country. You are free to leave.

If you want to "Freeload", complain, cause
descent, disregard our laws and rules, and in
general be a ner-do-well; if you want to change
our form of government because you think you
know better, please go and find another
country that has a government formed the way
you want it, but leave this one alone, we like it
the way it is.

In Article III (THE GOVERNMENT) an attempt
to formalize the type and extent of government
is made. A democratic republic for the country
at large and a republican government model
ensured for the several states.

It is truly unfortunate that the hubris and
arrogance found within the human animal is so
readily found in persons that have acquired
power. In the past this has been all too evident
in the persons that have been brought into
office in the Congress, the Presidency, and the
Supreme Court. If we could only find people of
the ilk of our founders once again, we could
install them for terms of many years without
worrying that they would demonstrate the

corruption we have so often found in our current lot of politicians.

It is necessary to find a way to spread the responsibility and power structure across the whole of the government with the several branches acting to keep each other focused on doing the good work our country needs and deserves. It has been seen recently that the President, the Congress, nor the Supreme Court can be relied upon to work solely in the best interest of the people and the country.

The President has been shown to act more like a dictator when given enough reins, the Congress will collude amongst themselves and with the President to pass or forestall certain legislative actions, the Supreme Court acts on personal "feelings", the writings and philosophies and interpretations of foreign governments or from some personal desire to either advance or derail the arguments presented before it.

The idea of trusting the Government to work in the best interest of the country and its citizens has been lost in great part and a change must be made to find a way back to a society and government that will work together and once again begin a healing process, so sorely needed.

It is necessary to call an end to the Congress at the end of this last session and remove the Justices from the Supreme Court; remove the President and Vice-President and replace them with a governing council of while a constitutional convention is brought forth to review this new version of the Constitution with the changes in the governmental organization and ratify it so we can once again move forward as the great nation we once were.

No violence is needed nor will it be allowed; the Department of Defense, police forces, the states, the homeland security departments and other essential governmental functions shall remain in place and working as they are now. This is not a coup but a re-organization, a rebirth without the violence that was necessary in order to obtain our initial independence. We are still a free and independent nation with an elected government based on a democratic republican form.

It is essential that the citizenry be ensured that they will be fine and their voices will be heard during the transition. They are asked to refrain from overt and extreme actions but to instead be patient and talk among themselves to begin a healing process in their communities. They can begin considering ways they may improve their towns and cities; to harness the good and eliminate the bad.

The Convention will work through a six month period and massage the contents of this new constitution and governmental organization into a "well-oiled" machine and the new government transition can be put in place with the changes being made as quickly as is found to be practical, but all departmental changes shall be made within a twelve (12) month period of time.

The social programs may phase out over a period of two or three years; the foreign and other non-essential distribution of monies from the Treasury (the taxpayers) shall end immediately.

If a governmental department is eliminated during the re-organization, any rules and regulations promulgated under its authority are placed on hold pending a comprehensive review whereafter they shall be moved to another department or eliminated as the case may be.

Elections among the several states to form the new Congress and a new President shall be held within six (6) months of the ratification process and they shall be installed within two (2) months thereafter.

The formation and maintenance of military, naval, and even the forward looking "space-borne" forces is mentioned as a necessary accompaniment for any national government to consider for the present and future survival. While it is desirous to never have a need for such preparations, still it must be done. If the forces are so well trained, so well equipped, and so terrible in their effectiveness that foreign adversaries would regret warranting their attention; effectively remanding it to the status of a "defense" force for all intents and purposes.

The government is called upon to be the voice of the nation with respect to international relationships and co-operation; for global commerce, security, and diplomatic considerations. This international aspect of the government is under the auspices of the Executive Branch presided over by the President of the United States.

The internal portion of the governments responsibilities now fall to the Branch of "Operations" which is burdened with the functioning of the Federal Government from the border to all internal infrastructure, and to maintain close communications and assistance with the several states, territories, and possessions.

Another new branch for the government is the "Legal and Security" Branch which shall have the Attorney General's office and the Security Director's office under the Branch Chief.

The most important feature of these two branches is that they will work completely without political color. No manner of preference or discrimination shall be met upon the populace with regard to any personal description other than the status of citizen or resident alien.

One of the primary divisions within this Branch is that of the Attorney General, whose task is to work with the Security Division in investigating and gathering information for submission to the courts for the purposes of enforcement of the nations laws.

Another of the primary and most significant roles for the branch is the border security and treating breaches in our borders with great prejudice indeed. For one to define a country it is essential that the "borders" are a key component of the description, and without that the idea of "country" does not apply at all.

Yet another primary role is the security of the country "within". This involves the close cooperation and communications with all state and regional law enforcement agencies and departments. Gathering data by various means and sharing it with all departments and agencies that may be affected by it in a fast and effective way will be essential.

With the large volume of travellers coming in from abroad as well as those residing and travelling within the country's borders; the need for excellent tracking, reporting, and communications is of the utmost importance.

The powers and authority conferred upon the Federal Government is by the citizens; the governed are the "employers" of the government and the employees thereof. Likewise the states derive their authority and power to govern from the same citizenry on a regional and local level. For the nation under this type of structure, the voice of the people must be heard.

Any attempts to keep them without a voice is in violation of the precepts contingent herein and the perpetrator of such behavior must be removed from any position of power or authority by whatever means is necessary to accomplish the task. It is obvious that a peaceful means is preferred for such an effort.

The government personnel, including the elected, selected, recruited, or employed, are EMPLOYEES of the people of the United States and serve at their discretion. Do the jobs you are hired to do, do them well. Ensure your work stays within the laws given by the Constitution and remember that you are "one of many".

Since the employees of the government, and thereby of the citizens, are required to serve in their capacity as hired, no type of labor, professional, or trade unions are allowed. Any grievances by any employee shall be made and attended to by the appropriate chain of management. Valid claims of mistreatment or abusive procedures are to be corrected without undue delay.

While no formal educational, health care or retirement benefits are included as a part of their employment, certain job related training programs may be provided, "sick" leave is also included and the employees are encouraged, but not required, to participate in a "self-directed" and funded retirement program. Vacation leave is also a part of the benefits provided.

In order to ensure the longevity of the society and its governmental model, it is essential that the expenditures of the federal government do not exceed the revenues collected for any particular period of time. The level of federal expenditures should be firmly restricted to a portion of the National GDP that does not exceed 12 percent.

There are possible times ahead wherein a national or regional crisis, perhaps even war, will require a temporary increase in expenditures. When such difficulties pass, the federal and state/regional governments must return the modest spending levels to their original amounts and also replenish the funds to the government coffers that have been utilized during the time of distress.

Care must be used in all our financial dealings and in controlling expenditures, and perhaps a means to set aside a fund to be used in such times of crisis.

Reckless attempts by the government authority to exaggerate the status of the financial condition of the nation by printing excessive amounts of currency are to be avoided. Any debts or agreements in international commerce as well as domestic transactions require a stable and reasonably valued currency.

Since such a value is a direct reflection of the economic stability and status of the national economy, it is highly desirous that the economic model of the nation as a whole, the several states, and the productivity of the citizenry be jealously upheld and encouraged to thrive.

Undue regulations, rules, procedures, policies promulgated by any government, national or lesser, must be rebuked and not allowed to occur. As has occurred in the past, such actions have been seen, even at the highest levels of government, and in great part due to the pressure brought to bear by "special interest" groups, persons, ideals, or influential parties. Such attempts may very well have been of laudable goals and undeniably highly desirable potential results but nonetheless without sufficient basis in fact of science to warrant governmental action.

The ability of the various government "agencies", departments, divisions, or other groups of whatever type to introduce their own rules and pseudo "Legislation" for the public to follow is withdrawn. They will no longer have the right to introduce by rule, direction, or statute, or any other mechanism their idea of how things should work. If legislation is needed in order for them to accomplish their tasks, they must go through the congress to arrange for it through proper channels.

Heretofore, these departments and agencies have promulgated their own idea of rules and regulations with statutory authority; legislating, if you will. Some also had their own enforcement personnel and some would pass judgments and award penalties to the offenders. That is not in accord with the principles of this constitution and is not sanctioned.

Care must be taken to withhold such actions that may be due to the excitement of the moment and must be based on a clear concept of the desired end result and a sure a carefully planned course of action. Too many times has it been found that similar actions, well meaning in concept, have resulted in excessive expenditures, harsh and devastating effects on industries, and damaging or completely destroying private companies, individuals, and communities through economic hardships sustained.

To hear some advocates voice their tirades, it would be taken that there are those in business of general society that advocate for a dirty planet, harsh pollution, destruction of an animal species, or other notorious desires. Mores the pity that they are of so vociferous and contentious demeanor; even worse that

that is that many people that hear their rants are so poorly educated or ignorant of the base arguments that they follow along as if such declarations are fact and indeed foretell of dire results.

While these "advocates" have the right to speak their minds, whatever their motives may be, they should be confronted with opposing or alternative approaches in order to satisfy the unease that they so often inflict upon the general population. If their voice and irresponsible presentation of "facts" subsequently causes harm, damage, of otherwise injures persons or businesses wellbeing, steps must be allowed and indeed, encouraged to compensate them by the person or persons that have incited and thus caused the damages.

In Article IV (THE EXECUTIVE BRANCH) an attempt is brought forth to lay further definition on the Executive Branch of the government and relieve the overwhelming level of responsibility that has caused a confused, if not unwieldy, activity by the President in dealing with all the needs of the nation. It has been proven that the larger the nation has become, the more attention it must demand of the governmental machine. To alleviate such pressures and thus ensure that all international and domestic obligations are sufficiently attended to, a forth branch of Government is introduced to further address the needs of the nation.

The term in office is limited to a single six (6) year term. No further need shall exist for the "President" to expend time, monies, or energies in activities involving elections for themselves or other political candidates. The use of government facilities, equipment, or personnel for such activities is expressly forbidden.

The Executive Branch is responsible strictly for the international business of the nation. This will include all communications, negotiations, and necessary responses to crises, planning of international actions and activities, and hosting diplomats of foreign nations that may visit here.

The departments the President has under him are:

The Department of State
The Department of Defense
The Central Intelligence Agency
The Department for International Commerce
The Office of the United States Attorney

The Secretary of State reports to the President and is responsible for overall international diplomatic functions: Initial contacts with foreign entities, treaty negotiations, and peaceful conflict resolutions through diplomatic means, strategic positioning and the like. The state department is responsible for passports, visas, and vetting of foreign visitors for entry into the country for extended periods of study or work.

The Department of Defense is the organization of and for the various armed forces of the country under which they are organized. The Secretary of Defense works under the President to maintain a cohesive and ordered action strategy for all foreign engagements.

The department senior officers of the various services shall form the Joint Chief of Staff, which Group shall include the senior most officer from the National Guard, Air National Guard, and Merchant Marine, if activated. The Chairman of the Joint Chiefs shall be the senior most member of this group and serve for a period of three (3) years, eligible for more terms if foreign actions are in process.

The several services shall recruit, staff, train, and equip the personnel that serve within their branch of service. The Department shall work with American businesses, research and development groups, and academia to ensure the highest possible level of quality and sophistication of all equipment, materials, and supplies needed in support of their missions.

The various Services shall evaluate their needs for capital equipment on an ongoing basis and monitor the "State-of-the-Art" for all technologies involved in the concepts, design, and fabrication of these assets.

While fundamental research and development operations in our various industries is important to the end result for our weaponry and supportive equipment, prudent cost analysis and expenditures is essential to maintain efficiency for the dollar amounts expended.

Contracts with companies for specific research or development projects must be well defined, with specific goals and performance criteria.

Time schedules and expenditures are to be well controlled and care must be taken to ensure timely and "On-Budget" performance of the contracts.

All information gathered during deployments is to be transmitted to the National Security Agency for archiving and dissemination to other governmental groups that may be affected by it. All information and communications of the department shall be considered classified.

Close co-operation with the other departments of the Executive Branch is essential and must include full communications at the highest levels.

The President is still the Commander-in-Chief of the military, naval, air, and space-borne forces, if any, and as such may request of Congress that a Declaration of War be pronounced in response to a hostile action by a foreign force, which action could not be avoided by diplomatic means.

Conversely the Congress may require of the President that he send an armed force to an area of conflict that has proven to be of concern as the security and national interest of the country may demand. The president may choose to require a meeting with the Congress before sending such a force but must prepare it upon conclusion of the meeting if the result of the meeting so requires.

The Central Intelligence Agency is responsible for all foreign intelligence-gathering operations. This includes all hiring of human resources, vetting of foreign nationals engaged in their service and equipping the field operating personnel with the best equipment available for their use.

The training, equipping, and posting of agents shall remain as covert as possible. Rosters and identities shall be withheld from public knowledge as much as possible. All data gathered shall be analyzed and the results reported to the Chief of the Agency for proper dissemination to the President, National Security Agency, and other governmental entities that may be affected by the information discovered. All data gathered shall be classified with an appropriate level and shared with the National Security Agency for archiving and internal action strategy planning.

The Department of International Commerce is responsible for the research and identification of commercial customers for the products and services available from our country's various commercial enterprises. The initial contacts and eventual negotiations on the governmental level will precede all subsequent "business level" interaction they may initiate. They are responsible for major trade agreements and the negotiation of top-level details that may have political or military implications.

The United States Attorneys office shall be responsible for keeping the various written communications, orders, judicial requests and filings with the Supreme Court, Requests of the Congress, and various other background documents and actions by the Executive Branch to be Constitutional and within the boundaries of the law.

This office is responsible for review of all congressional requests, communications from the Supreme Court, and preparing the written arguments for the Executive Position on various subjects.

This office is responsible for the legal response of the Executive Branch to any and all formal writs, injunctions, warrants, subpoenas, and actions presented to the Office of the President.

If a member of this branch is planning or otherwise required to present themselves to the Congress for a meeting or committee investigation, this department shall prepare and support that member with full background and statistical information as well as brief them on potential legal issues that may ensue. This office will have a representative accompany all members, thus involved in such presentations.

The President may solicit the Congress to provide sufficient funds be made available to support activities of the Executive Branch deemed necessary and lawful.

The President shall still have his voice present in the Senate in the person of the Vice President but while having the privilege of the floor, shall not have a vote on any bills or resolution under consideration or the vote.

In Article V (THE LEGISLATIVE BRANCH) We are discussing the Legislative Branch in greater detail. This branch has been traditionally involved in creating legislation for the purpose of making laws for the various functioning of the nation with a set of "rules" by which everyone can plan their activities in harmony with the rest of society.

It is sadly noted that this function is not particularly adept at also reviewing the past legislation efforts and culling out those "laws" that no longer are germane or practical to a society that is constantly changing. A separate committee should be thus set in action to constantly review the past works and recommend to the congress a plan of action for removal or possible modification of aging legislation.

The idea is that old and outdated laws still require the attention of the enforcement section of the Legal and Security Branch and thereby utilize time and costs unnecessarily. Removing such laws will tend to streamline the overall structure of the departments as well as improve efficiency.

Past experience has shown that the members of the Congress are highly aligned with political parties in their deliberations and actions; this propensity is not to the benefit of the country nor the people they are supposed to be serving. There have been some that have taken on the mantel of mini-dictator in driving the Senate and the House to do their particular bidding with respect to legislation. A complete renovation of the rules and procedures of both the House and Senate must be accomplished immediately.

In future congressional activities the use of term limits and requirements of the leadership offices will tend to moderate this action significantly. By requiring the Speaker of the

House and the President of the Senate to refer the proposed legislation to the floor, and not permitting it to be "withheld", the actions of the houses will move along in a more democratic way. A wider variety of legislations can be brought and considered. With changes in the rules of the floor and procedures, a congress with a higher calling to serve the best ideals of the country instead of themselves will be, at last, evident.

With the formal requirement of 66 percent of the members required in both houses in order for a legislation to pass into law, the impetus for a more deliberate and well thought out legislation will take place. With the President no longer involved in the passing of laws and not able to "veto" them, a more reasoned and deliberate approach to legislation is required. No "bill" can pass without the large majority and for that to occur, better communications between members will be essential. One political party will not have the ability to push bills on with a simple majority any longer.

Care should be taken to "hear" all members from the floor if they have an interest it the bill before them. The use of deterrent procedures and the filibuster is to be discouraged if good communications and attitude are put to good use. If we all speak with the good of the country in mind, but still speak our mind in an attempt to get our ideas aired, we have done a good thing.

A divisive attitude has existed in the past wherein there have been "Factions" that put themselves aside from the larger contingent. They are certain "special Interest" caucuses that either conspire or wish to simply not participate in the government as it was designed to function. The idea of these caucuses has a tendency to alienate others, cast suspicion and instill a distancing from the larger group. It seems counterproductive to the precept of working together as a whole to solve problems, and bring the results forth for the good of all.

If you insist on being "white", "Black", "Asian", "Christian", "Atheist", Democrat", Republican" or whatever, you are undermining the basis upon which we must rely in order to pull together. We are "AMERICANS" and should act like the adults we are and be proud of the country in which we live and thus proud of ourselves as well. If The Congress works under this set of ideals, it will better serve the nation and if it challenges any action in opposition, it will have done a good thing.

Likewise the selection of the Justices and Federal Judges alike shall be held as much as possible to be without political influence and the terms of all of their terms in service is finite by intent.

It is clear from past events that legislation must be created to establish a "blanket" of security across the nation. A means for close human and electronic surveillance of possible insurgents within our borders must be put in place; this will require a system of clandestine scrutinizing and pre-emptive intervention. This is, of course, a dangerous and controversial action; it defines a fine line between an abundance of caution and paranoia.

74

Since this type of legislation enters personal and private activities, it is essential that such legislation must be directed only at potentially dangerous activities and intentional conveyors of harm to our populous.

For ordinary enquiries, information and data gathering in actions typically in use by our law enforcement agencies, specific warrants must still be required.

In Article VI (THE OPERATIONS BRANCH) we are discussing the Operations Branch. This "NEW" Branch is an addition for the purpose of relieving the Executive Branch of such a broad range of responsibilities in its day-to-day operations as well as re-organize the levels of responsibility and authorities that have proved troublesome in the recent past.

Without question, the Congressional and the Presidential positions are politically driven. We have however found that fundamental conflict has arisen by virtue of the political content of these branches, "coloring" much of their functioning; not a good nor tenable situation within a just and responsible system of government.

It is seen as essential that these problem areas be addressed and an organizational and operational plan be put in place to remove the possibility of recurrence in the future.

To this end this forth branch is envisioned wherein it is completely without any political color in its functioning. There are no "elected" positions or "Presidential" appointees and all of its departments and agencies are held to function with the idea of no partisanship, favoritism, or derision for any group or persons.

The Operations Branch has the largest operating contingent of the Federal Government within its prevue. The various departments and Agencies from the past Executive Branch, if they remain, and not specifically functioning in the international service are thereby moved to within the umbrella of this branch.

All standard domestic functions that remain shall be organized hereunder. All shall function under the caution that they will act and perform without political color and see all citizens with the same personages with respect to interactions with them.

This Branch had no legislative responsibilities or powers. The Congress holds all legislative powers.

This branch is responsible for the support of all other government branches, departments, and groups for their needs in infrastructure maintenance and supportive activities such as transportation, buildings, internal investigations, needed material items, other supportive functions as may come to light.

This branch offers a close communications and data storehouse for all medical, drug, and disease information as well as the data bank for all other government activities. It is responsible for all federal transportation inspections, and services to the private and public transportation companies in the country.

This branch is responsible, in conjunction with the several states and territories for developing, improving, and maintaining the national infrastructure components such as major highways, dams, bridges, navigable waterways, federal communications systems, oversight concerning commercial and private pipelines, and other functional utilitarian interstate activities, and the like.

It is also responsible for all government data archiving and distribution as may be required from time-to-time. Such archiving activity shall be held under a triple redundancy security system with a revolving security key system. Only persons with the highest "Top Secret" clearance are allowed to enter or work in that area.

This branch is responsible to ensure that all contractors and workers that deal with any classified materials, even as low as "Confidential" are citizens of the United States and they themselves hold the proper credentials and clearances to be in or work within those areas. No persons who are citizens of, or are from, a country that has been or is currently classified as a belligerent country are allowed a clearance of any kind or of any level.

This branch is responsible for the government's technology, weights, measures, and engineering standards as well as maintaining a close relationship and communications with the engineering, medical, and scientific communities within the country

In Article VII **(THE LEGAL AND SECURITY BRANCH)** this branch has investigatory and prosecutorial responsibility in enforcing the laws of the land, and ***all*** of them.

The reason for the separation of the powers and responsibilities of this branch is to ensure the isolation from "political" influence in the operations residing within this branch. It is essential for the law enforcement and federal court system remain without color or involvement in the routine operations of the other branches; thus this branch is strictly involved in the investigations, the legal enforcement of federal laws, and the prosecution of persons, groups, or organizations accused of breaking those laws.

For any domestic function in which the Federal Government has a voice or primary responsibility, this branch has first level responsibility. All federal Law Enforcement, Intra-state activities, and federal infrastructure responsibilities rest here.

The Border Patrol, Federal Marshall Service, Federal Bureau of Investigation, Port Authority Enforcement, Secret Service, the Coast Guard during peacetime, and the National Security Agency are under this branch. All of their actions, efforts, investigative findings, enforcement actions, and communications are to be included within the national databank archives for safekeeping and sharing with other departments as may be needed.

A thorough and pro-active interaction with all other departments and agencies (and Branches) is the order of the day. Difficulties or perceived reluctance on the part of any other government group, or person should be reported and a resolution sought.

One of the key issues for its oversight is the Cyber Technology Agency; concerned with the utilization, misuse, and cyber crime incidents as they occur. Within the "Utilization" department, all cyber technologies shall be studied and developed to their maximum utility. They will become expert at all manner of cyber crime techniques, be responsible for intercepting all "hack attacks" from whatever source, and be responsible for tracking them back to their origins.

In Article VIII (THE JUDICIAL BRANCH) we introduce the Supreme Court with a few changes from the historical one we are all accustomed to. While we still seat nine (9) justices they are chosen in The Congress and each serves a total of nine (9) years if they remain physically and mentally competent for such duration and while being of good behavior.

An annual change in the makeup of the Supreme Court Justices will help to improve the non-political attitudes found there in the recent past.

The most senior Justice shall take the position of "Chief Justice" and be responsible for directing the day-to-day judicial activities of the court.

Each Justice shall have a personal staff of three (3) salaried assistants as well as having the Clerical Section at their disposal when needed.

A Chief Administrator will head up the support staff comprising the research, clerical, and inter-branch activities committee, and finally the Court Security staff. All incoming correspondence shall pass through the clerical section screening group; supported by a staff of attorneys as well as paralegals. Questions as to the "standing" of the party bringing action as well as appropriate content are decided here.

All personnel working within the Supreme Court building must qualify and hold a security clearance of secret or above. All employees must observe absolute confidentiality, and the Perimeter of the complex is to be manned by the Court Security staff at all times. All persons entering will pass a screening room wherein the identification and materials being transported are checked.

The Court Security section will have the courier group attached to it and all physical items being sent out or being received shall pass a screening regimen.

FINANCIAL (and other) CONSIDERATIONS

During the formation of the United States of America as we have known it from our history, the Federal Government was set up as the voice of the new nation with the explicit responsibility of security for the new nation and for being its voice for international purposes; The powers were bestowed upon it by the citizens, and those not explicitly given were to be held by the citizens themselves and the several states.

One of the most important items, and a key reason for the abandoning of the Articles of Confederation was the inability of the federal government to do business without a funding source. To this end the Constitution included the power of thee federal government to levy taxes and by other means enlist the states to fund the activities that had been given it.

Originally the states had continued to hold local governance powers. Suspicion was voiced in having a strong central government for fear that it would eventually grow too large in size and power and become essentially a tyrannical master.

There have been occasional hints of that beginning to occur and perhaps its time to once again demonstrate the desire of the states and citizens to address the issue of conferred powers and responsibilities.

To this end the re-organization and streamlining of the Branches of Government and governmental system, and this accompanied by a financial plan whereby the Federal Government once again dedicates it efforts and facilities to the tasks of national security, international dealings, and a general administering partner to ensure the continued national coalescence of the several states, possessions and territories.

Further to this end the following thoughts are tendered to consider a financial approach to ensure the continued local governmental positions while concurrently ensuring a reasonable mechanism for the continued funding for the national government.

For the first year, all taxation shall remain as it is at the present time while the federal and various state governments prepare for the transition into the new one. The various state governments already have a taxing structure in place and the changes are expected to be a matter of scaling it up and then allowing for an introduction of the various "state and local" functions back to their control. They are encouraged to effect the transition as soon as possible; the Federal Government shall give full support during the transition.

In lieu of this change in taxing structure, the states, possessions, and territories will be responsible for the taxing of their domestically located businesses and residents as they may see fit to do; the states and territories shall be the conduit through which the Federal Government receives its primary revenue stream.

That primary funding of the Federal Government shall be accomplished through a taxing structure that relies on the several states and territories themselves. A secondary stream of revenues shall come from fees, duties, interest received, and taxes on foreign transactions, businesses, and persons living abroad, excise taxes and other miscellaneous receipts.

The Federal Government shall collect no income, payroll, capital gains, inheritance, or gift taxes, from its citizens living within the United States or it's territories.

No federal taxes shall be levied against any income earned by domestically based business from domestic operations; a federal tax on all monies brought into the country by domestically based companies from international operations will be at a rate, not to exceed 5%. All monies earned by internationally based businesses from operations within this country or its territories shall be taxed at the rate of 15%.

If a domestic company has a manufacturing facility or partial ownership of such a facility overseas; all products that are manufactured by those facilities and imported into the United States shall pay a minimum import tariff of 20%. If such products or services are in competition, direct or indirect, with a domestic company, the minimum tariff is set at 30%.

The Federal Government will calculate the revenues owed by each state as a function of their entire adult population and a percentage of the state or territory's Average Per Capita GSP. The calculations shall be made on a quarterly basis. The revenue payment shall be on a quarterly basis as well.

The use of the term "entire" means to include the present transient population including all homeless, indigent, and those identifiable as illegally in the United States and residing there either temporarily or "permanently"; it must also include all persons that are presently working and residing (including DoD personnel) within that state or territory even though they are "permanent" citizens of another.

The weighted calculations favor a more industrious populace, not necessarily one of a manufacturing type but simply an industrious one. For a society with a significant percentage of "welfare" recipients or "wards-of-the-state", the costs will prove to be proportionally higher than one in which everyone is "pulling" their own weight.

The matrix used for the calculations will "see" the hard (and smart) working agrarian community scoring as well as a highly labor-intensive manufacturing one. Non-working and non-productive adults are still counted as adult persons for the purpose of a per capita calculation of a society.

The calculations and revenue amounts are based on the current state and national demographics for which an annual running census is required on the 1) Number of citizens resident, 2) the number of citizens between the ages of 18 an 70 years of age, 3) the number of non-citizen residents including all permanent, temporary, and those residing here illegally. The term "illegally" includes any person residing there that is not a citizen and is not registered as a temporary student, temporary worker, or legal permanent non-citizen resident; including all such adults and minors.

The present (2016) Annual Federal Budget is: ~$B 3.2, WOW! But its expenditures are over $B 3.9!!!!! The total state and territory GSP is: ~$B 17.905

It is desirous that the Federal Government "collects" as little revenue as possible in order to accomplish its tasks. The states and territories would no doubt applaud this, as would the populace.

The current outlay and costs of $B 3.9 would be substantially reduced with the forthcoming re-organization of the Governmental system. Fully one half of the present federal departments, agencies and offices would be closed and their tasks would be transferred to a state level responsibility among with the various structures, buildings, equipment, and probably the personnel as well.

The planned task structure for the remaining federal programs would realize an overall cut in efforts, responsibilities, authority, and funding.

Eventually the Federal Government shall not provide medical, educational, welfare, tuition, or other financial benefits directly to the citizens; they will have to rely on their state, possession, or territorial governments for the benefits they receive, if any.

Maintenance, support, and operational budgets would drop sharply. With the total welfare and entitlement expenditures removed, the total budget would be expected to be at a maximum level of ~$B1.1. The burdens on the individual taxpayers to their states would diminish by half and the states, with much less financial burden due to a much higher efficiency of operations on the local level would thrive once again.

The Federal Government will phase out the Social Security and the Medicare benefits programs within a five (5) year period; they shall be transferred to the states. It is envisioned that the social security and Medicare program out-phasing will include a form of "Lump Sum" payout in view of the annual contributions collected by the Federal Government from the beneficiaries. The calculations of the lump sums involved will be complex and the formula for those calculations will be presented to all concerned before the programs are initiated.

A sample of the program phase-out of the social security assistance may be similar to this:

1. Persons that are 50 years of age or less must arrange for their own retirement coverage. The states, and local government may wish to set up a co-ordination effort or offer an investment plan.

2. A lump sum payment intended to return a portion of the funds contributed by way of employment deductions, if any, shall be calculated. If the state in which a person resides is chosen by the citizen to take the place of the federal program, this payment will transfer to the state and the only changes to affect the citizens will be within the state controls; alternatively the payment shall go to the person and they would be responsible for getting their own retirement coverage thereafter.

3. Perhaps the calculation would appear like so:

$$\$R = N*\$C*DS$$
$$\$R = \text{(dollars returned)}$$
$$N = \text{Number of Years paid}$$
$$\$C = \text{(contribution per year)}$$
$$DS = \text{depreciation schedule}$$

4. The "Depreciation Schedule" will take into account, the contributions made, the amount of payments already distributed, the country's economic condition, and the recipients' means to subsist without further assistance.

The Department of Health and Human Services, Education, Interior, Energy, and Labor will be terminated; any essential functions as well as ongoing contracts and R&D projects are to be reviewed and transferred to an appropriate surviving department.

The Internal Revenue Service work force will be reduced by 95 percent and incorporated within the new Department of the Treasury, the Environmental Protection Agency shall be terminated and the regulations promulgated by it shall be set aside pending formal review.

A review of the mission, activities, and function of all remaining departments and agencies will be conducted at once and redundancy in those areas eliminated. A significant reduction in force is required.

The National Park Service shall be disbanded and the National Parks placed under the state, possession, or territory in which they are located; for national parks that are encompassed by the boundaries of two or more states, those states will be "stewards-in-common" and expected to act together to ensure a continuing high standard of repair and presentation as well as good access by the general public.

The states, possessions, and territories are encouraged to begin a transition preparation effort immediately. The use of the "free market" approach to both the "Medicare" and "Social Security" programs is strongly recommended, and with the help of the local governments, the transition should not be traumatic.

www.ingramcontent.com/pod-product-compliance
Lightning Source LLC
Chambersburg PA
CBHW070835310526
45788CB00017B/1209